A View From 151st Street

by

Bob Glaudini

New York Hollywood London Toronto

SAMUELFRENCH.COM

Copyright © 2008 by Bob Glaudini

ALL RIGHTS RESERVED

CAUTION: Professionals and amateurs are hereby warned that *A VIEW FROM 151ST STREET* is subject to a royalty. It is fully protected under the copyright laws of the United States of America, the British Commonwealth, including Canada, and all other countries of the Copyright Union. All rights, including professional, amateur, motion picture, recitation, lecturing, public reading, radio broadcasting, television and the rights of translation into foreign languages are strictly reserved. In its present form the play is dedicated to the reading public only.

The amateur live stage performance rights to *A VIEW FROM 151ST STREET* are controlled exclusively by Samuel French, Inc., and royalty arrangements and licenses must be secured well in advance of presentation. PLEASE NOTE that amateur royalty fees are set upon application in accordance with your producing circumstances. When applying for a royalty quotation and license please give us the number of performances intended, dates of production, your seating capacity and admission fee. Royalties are payable one week before the opening performance of the play to Samuel French, Inc., at 45 W. 25th Street, New York, NY 10010.

Royalty of the required amount must be paid whether the play is presented for charity or gain and whether or not admission is charged.

Stock royalty quoted upon application to Samuel French, Inc.

For all other rights than those stipulated above, apply to: ICM, 825 Eighth Avenue, New York, NY 10019 Attn: Thomas Pearson.

Particular emphasis is laid on the question of amateur or professional readings, permission and terms for which must be secured in writing from Samuel French, Inc.

Copying from this book in whole or in part is strictly forbidden by law, and the right of performance is not transferable.

Whenever the play is produced the following notice must appear on all programs, printing and advertising for the play: "Produced by special arrangement with Samuel French, Inc."

Due authorship credit must be given on all programs, printing and advertising for the play.

ISBN 978-0-573-66275-1   Printed in U.S.A.   #24648

No one shall commit or authorize any act or omission by which the copyright of, or the right to copyright, this play may be impaired.

No one shall make any changes in this play for the purpose of production.

Publication of this play does not imply availability for performance. Both amateurs and professionals considering a production are strongly advised in their own interests to apply to Samuel French, Inc., for written permission before starting rehearsals, advertising, or booking a theatre.

No part of this book may be reproduced, stored in a retrieval system, or transmitted in any form, by any means, now known or yet to be invented, including mechanical, electronic, photocopying, recording, videotaping, or otherwise, without the prior written permission of the publisher.

IMPORTANT BILLING AND CREDIT REQUIREMENTS

All producers of *A VIEW FROM 151ST STREET* *must* give credit to the Author of the Play in all programs distributed in connection with performances of the Play, and in all instances in which the title of the Play appears for the purposes of advertising, publicizing or otherwise exploiting the Play and/or a production. The name of the Author *must* appear on a separate line on which no other name appears, immediately following the title and *must* appear in size of type not less than fifty percent of the size of the title type.

A VIEW FROM 151ST STREET was originally produced by the LAByrinth Theater Company at the Public Theater. It opened on October 18, 2007. It was directed by Peter Dubois, and assistant directed by Damon Arrington.

The original cast featured:

DWIGHT	Gbenga Akinnagbe
LENA	Liza Colón-Zayas
DELROY	Craig "muMs" Grant
DANIEL	Juan Carlos Hernandez
MONROE	Russell G. Jones
MARA	Marisa Malone
IRENE	Elizabeth Rodriguez
RAY	Andre Royo

TIME

The Present.

PLACE

New York City.

SET

Main set: front room of the Prats apartment.

Other areas: Corner of West 151 Street and Broadway, a bed area in VA hospital, an empty city lot, 148th st area, front gate of a construction yard.

A trio: Stand up bass, guitar, sax– in view off to the side of stage.

ACT ONE

Scene 1

(West 151 & Broadway. Music. Breaks off. **DELROY** *and* **DANIEL**. **DANIEL** *has a grape soda.)*

(Dialogue immediate, heated.)

DELROY. If I say it gonna happen, nigga, it gonna happen!

DANIEL. I can't fuck with my money nigga!

DELROY. Y'don't listen!

DANIEL. I know what y'tryin to say!

DELROY. You don't know what I say till I say it!

DANIEL. He don't wait forever, B.

DELROY. He go where he want, B. But this shit comin, y'don't jump on it 10 times, y'give a white nigga heart attack.

DANIEL. I don't get between my nigga n' somethin don't happen.

DELROY. Y'got to shut the fuck up'n listen!

DANIEL. It mess up, it mess me up!

DELROY. Be a man, or suck my dick while I drink my grape soda!

DANIEL. My money nigga wanna *supersize*, B!

DELROY. My DR nigga wantya do business with me on a quarter to prove you right. Only be 5 n' some.

DANIEL. 5 n' some?

DELROY. The shit gonna be pure, B.

DANIEL. Shit pure, he on it.

DELROY. Y'turn a quarter first, shit get here, y'nigga meet my nigga n'supersize all he want.

DANIEL. I gotta know when, B.

DELROY. Shit leavin on donkeys n'shit to cross the muthafukan ocean n'shit!

DANIEL. You keep sayin –

DELROY. I know what the fuck I say! Don't say what I say back at me! Y'show y'real, then *I-O-U*, muthafuka, cuz I get my cake to buy tracks from my nigga, Fat Spanky, know what I'm sayin? My flavor need to fly live on Shade 45. DJ Kay Slay, Drama King, shout it to the world, B. "Killa Crisis in the house!" Arright. Talk to y'nigga. I'm busy now.

DANIEL. I be with you.

DELROY. I be here.

> (*DANIEL exits. DELROY adjusts his earphones. Improvises the sound of beats. A mumble*) Lock the flavor down.
>
> (*little stronger*)
>
> Lookit, mom, this is what. Listen up, mom, go like… shit that some shit –
>
> (*Music.*)
>
> (*raps, still to himself*)
>
> I'm chillin in a buildin
> while a bust get run
> cops r'lining up my niggas
> on 1-51
> yelling "hands on y'head, do it like done"
> 'nother day in Harlem havin fun
>
> (*breaks from rap*)
>
> Where my fucken addicts at? Shit.
>
> (*improvises beats, raps*)
>
> cops lick the rock
> MOBville niggas got

n'the DA won't see none of it
DRs gonna sling the shit
Mickey D's down onefortyfifth
Police say they keep 'em fit

(breaks from rap)

Muthafuken undependable ass dope fiends. Shit.

(improvises beats, thinks of rhymes)

Lick... fit... o-bit... or-bit...

(kicks it up)

Crisis gonna get in orbit
Gonna get wicked makin' obits
When he hear it

gonna G-up
get high
turn Santana way up
gonna roll in the tinted to the arches do a take-out
whatcha got
whatcha want
#1 Dominican
hommies on the side
pay y'out the window with a tec
pop-a-pop
take a tip from my clip
muthafukas gonna drop
pop-a-pop pop pop
Muthafukas down
Blood on the ground
Crisis gone like he come
back to the block
chillin in a buildin on 151
'nother day in Harlem with my homies havin fun
Killa Crisis! Doin his gangsta on Shade 45. Killllaaa...!

(Music builds into)

Scene 2

*(VA Hospital. **RAY** sits on the edge of the Bed, IV in place, hospital gown. **MARA** enters with a pill trolly.)*

MARA. How are you? Huh? Like shit?

RAY. I need some Klonopin.

MARA. I have medication for you.

RAY. What is it?

MARA. Propranolol.

RAY. I want Klonopin.

MARA. Propranolol is stronger.

RAY. *(accepts it)* Stronger?

MARA. Your friend's here.

RAY. I don't know no friend.

MARA. He's with the doctor. He asked could we find a rehab bed for you.

RAY. What the fuck y'talkin about?

MARA. The detective.

RAY. What detective?

MARA. Prats.

RAY. Say what?

MARA. The name you gave in case of death.

RAY. …shit… "in case of death?"

MARA. Prats. You don't remember him? You were in the army together. Daniel Prats.

RAY. …shit better be here…Prats, a detective, shit…

(finds a medal, rubs it for luck)

My good luck medal.

MARA. I think so, because we found a 90 day bed for you.

RAY. I can't do no rehab.

MARA. You were dead. You want to go back to finish the job?

RAY. Y'from Germany?

MARA. No.

RAY. Poland, somethin'.

MARA. Russia.

RAY. I can't get no American nurse in a VA Hospital?

MARA. I'm American citizen.

RAY. How come everyone we fight ends up workin' here?

MARA. At VA?

RAY. At USA. Every fucked up country. Next things you're workin' here.

MARA. If you want to quit crack, I listen to bullshit. If not – no way.

RAY. Y'know, fuck you.

MARA. *(matter of fact)* Fuck you, too....

(exiting)

Try not to shit your pants when you puke and cry like baby.

RAY. *(watching her go)* Shows what y'don't know. Kicking is in the mind. Dumb Russian. Crack is in the mind. Hell's gonna fall on me.

(Music. DANIEL enters unseen, observes RAY a moment. Music fades.)

DANIEL. Cutter.

RAY. *(under his breath)* ...man...Prats...

DANIEL. *(keeps a distance)* ...been a while, huh?

RAY. I don't remember givin them your name, y'know, under "who might care."

DANIEL. No matter. So, what's up?

RAY. I'm good.

DANIEL. You took the game too far.

RAY. Yeah, well...Y'a cop – they say?

DANIEL. Narcotics.

RAY. ...yeah...shit...

DANIEL. How long you been in New York?

RAY. Some.

DANIEL. Where you keep yourself?

RAY. Uptown some. Harlem. Westside. Nowhere special.

DANIEL. You run across a corner dealer named Delroy?

RAY. Delroy? Naw.

DANIEL. Works on a corner at West 151 and Broadway?

RAY. Naw, man.

DANIEL. He claims to huddle with the 151 MOBville set. M-O-B?

(*pause*)

Money Over Bitches?

RAY. No…

DANIEL. Delroy?

RAY. I don't know the nigga, arright?

DANIEL. Sorry, man. I'm a cop. I had to give it a shot.

RAY. The shot they gave me's coming on.

DANIEL. You know what? You do the 90. Hear it? Do 90. Keep clean. I'll help you get on your feet.

RAY. …This nigga's about to go out.

(**RAY** *fades, extends his fist.* **DANIEL** *taps it with his, exits.* **RAY** *sits up, broods. Music.*)

Scene 3

(West 151 & Broadway. **DELROY** *has earphones around his neck. Music fades.)*

DELROY. *(neutral, to himself)*
On the corner
Whatcha got
Whatcha want...

DWIGHT *(offstage) (down the block)* Hey you black ass nigga! You betta go off my block!

DELROY. *(shouts back)* Fuck you, n' suck my dick, nigga!

DWIGHT *(offstage) (enters)* I'm gonna shoot y'in the head, nigga!

DELROY. Hey, my nigga.

DWIGHT. Not bad.

(They do their handshake.)

DELROY. Better some addicts wake up.

DWIGHT. Maybe y'hit a pipe, they roll out they smell it.

DELROY. I off the rock, B, till I buy some beats for my demo.

DWIGHT. You got to *hold* money, B.

DELROY. That's why I off.

DWIGHT. Beats be more than the little you hold by steppin off.

DELROY. Ain't the only thing I'm gonna do for money, B.

DWIGHT. Arright. I'm gonna get a Philly down Mike's. You get with it?

DELROY. Get a Dutchie. Phillies down Mike's old n' crumble n'shit. Get a Dutch Vanilla they got 'em. Or honey flavor, they don't.

DWIGHT. *(exiting)* Arright.

DELROY. *(neutral to himself)*
On the corner here y'niggas cum
whatcha got

whatcha y'want

(calls to Dwight)

Dwight! Dwight!

(beat)

Fuckin nigga.

(calls again)

Dwight! Get me a loose!

DWIGHT *(off stage)* What?

DELROY. A loosie! Ma-bora!

DWIGHT. *(off stage)* Arright!!

DELROY. N'get n'orange juice!

DWIGHT. *(off stage)* What?

DELROY. A 50 cent box a orange juice! Deaf, ladycop-type-dyke, thick lip faggot muthafuka!

DWIGHT. *(off stage)* I'm gonna murder y'black nigga ass!

DELROY. I love you, my nigga! You know I love you!

(Music. Raps to himself, puts some on it)

On the corner

here y'niggas cum,

whatcha got

whatcha y'want

y'think i'm with y'but I'm in my mind lookin for a word got the flavor make my rhyme chime.

like it ice in my diamond mine.

(talks quietly)

Always ridin fresh Benzees. Bitches n' weed n' Cristal n' always strapped… Killlllllaaaa….

(Music out.)

Scene 4

(Front room. LENA gets school supplies together.)

DANIEL. *(entering)* Come on, we talked about it.

LENA. I know, but it's actually happening.

DANIEL. He'll sleep in the room I keep the weights in.

LENA. It's a closet.

DANIEL. They didn't call it a closet when we were looking.

LENA. "1.5 bedrooms."

DANIEL. He'll be grateful.

LENA. How long was rehab?

DANIEL. You forget what we talk about.

LENA. So how long was it?

DANIEL. What?

LENA. Rehab.

DANIEL. 90 days.

LENA. You haven't mentioned it. I thought he went back to doing what crack heads do best. Forget it. What else you got going?

DANIEL. What happen'd?

LENA. Some shit's going on, right?

DANIEL. Nothing's going on.

LENA. You're psyched all morning.

DANIEL. I go to the VA and pick him up. Bring him here. Then, it's just another day at work.

(He takes a gun out of a locked box.)

LENA. I don't like to see that out here.

DANIEL. What?

LENA. In the living room.

DANIEL. I don't complain about your job shit in here.

LENA. Water colors?

DANIEL. I'm gonna help him find a job and a room somewhere. He don't stay right, he's out the door. A week, four days. Probably less. Ok?

LENA. It's the way it is.

DANIEL. Word.

LENA. "Word?"

DANIEL. You don't bring home what you hear at work?

LENA. I teach ten year olds.

DANIEL. East Harlem.

LENA. What's that supposed to mean?

DANIEL. Nothing. You hooking up with my sister after work?

LENA. I think so.

DANIEL. She'll have an opinion.

LENA. No shit.

DANIEL. Ok. I'm gone.

LENA. Me too.

(Music.)

Scene 5

(West 151 & Broadway. **DELROY, DWIGHT.** **DELROY** *is concentrated on creating his rhymes.)*

DELROY. ...My nuts hang
I'm the nigga on the mike y'wanna shotta to bang...

DWIGHT. Nigga I'm tired waitin.

DELROY. *(ignores him)* ...my crunch make the bitches cling.

DWIGHT. Nigga, I ain't standin here all day like a bitch.

DELROY. Dwight, shit –

DWIGHT. Nigga, you ax to see me.

DELROY. Y'can't see what I'm doin?

DWIGHT. Y'ax'd to see me, nigga.

DELROY. I'm workin on a dis, B.

DWIGHT. Who you the fuck you gonna dis?

DELROY. I don't know yet, nigga.

DWIGHT. Uh-huh.

DELROY. If you were somebody people knew about, I'd dis you, muthafuka. Ya a faggot like that.

DWIGHT. Well bring your weak shit on.

DELROY. *(sounds some beats)* Lookit, mom, go like –

(sounds some beats. Music.)

I see y'talkin with y'posse in the Magic Johnson lobby
Sayin King Kong take on
Batman Spiderman Superman.
He that strong.
Y'a faggot like that!
King Kong too dumb t'get outta
Gameboy Blade 2 level 1.
They make Kong wrong.
He a fake King Kong.
They didn't give the nigga nuts
n'he got no dick.
Any fool know Kong got nuts

weigh a ton n'a dick a block long.
Y'a faggot like that!
Y'bitch say y'a faggot like that with nothin goin on
she laugh at y'shit while she up n'down on my dome.

DWIGHT. Ohhhh! That's some shit, my nigga!

DELROY. Why y'think I put down the stem?

DWIGHT. Arright.

DELROY. Keep my mind focused!

DWIGHT. Uh-huh. Y'say so.

DELROY. What?

DWIGHT. Y'say so.

DELROY. What you sayin?

DWIGHT. Saying y'say so s'all.

DELROY. I say so, cuz it is so!

DWIGHT. Uh-huh. I know what y'tryin to say.

DELROY. I'm not tryin to say it, muthafuka. I said it! I love ya, my nigga, y'know I love you, we been like brothers since y'wuz seven, but y'ignorant nigga sometime. The nigga, Fat Spanky, do beats for Dipset, stay on 151, other side of Broadway, n' he gonna work sump'n for my demo. So I need my mind focused.

DWIGHT. Uh-huh.

DELROY. Don't say "uh-huh" like y'a nigga from Africa. Santana come up on 151. Fat Spanky come up with him.

DWIGHT. I dinnit know Santana come up there.

DELROY. Cam'ron, lot a Dipset niggas. Niggas on the corners, Money Over Bitches niggas huddle for Diplomat.

DWIGHT. Them niggas front they bloods. Y'should located y'work on 1-48 n'Amsterdam with real black niggas.

DELROY. Fuck'yall sayin?

DWIGHT. I ax'd a nigga here had fuckin red around his head, red fuckin LA Clips jersey, red drawers under his red work outs. Nigga looked like he painted his sneaks in red paint – I ax'd who his OG is, he back off like a bitch.

DELROY. What nigga, my nigga?

DWIGHT. I ax'd who y'set, nigga? He stand there like he forgot how to talk, staring in space – I slap the bitch, who y'set nigga?

DELROY. Nigga, I ax'd what nigga you ax'd?

DWIGHT. The nigga got a big jaw, always have his mouth open.

DELROY. Fishface?

DWIGHT. I didn't ax the nigga's name.

DELROY. Fishface a mentally challenged retard nigga. Fishface ain't nothin. But step back from Dipset. They niggas I need to get with, B. Ya shit fall on me, y'dis Dipset.

DWIGHT. They all fools claim niggas.

DELROY. Dipset do shit. They don't do it, they get it done.

DWIGHT. Any nigga with money get a nigga with a gun to kill a nigga.

DELROY. That's what I'm sayin.

DWIGHT. Y'know them niggas?

DELROY. I wouldn't be here, I dinnit. It this side Broadway, not Mobville side, but it 151. Shit, I get with Fat Spanky once we get the money – tonight.

DWIGHT. Tonight?

DELROY. That nigga buy rock, I told 100 percent coke comin? Nigga believe it. I telling him shit a month, keep him comin' back –

DWIGHT. More than a month, B, cuz Florida fucked over UCLA then.

DELROY. My mind knows time, Dwight.

DWIGHT. You told me about the nigga when Florida killed UCLA. Your dumb ass thought UCLA faggots was gonna do somethin'. You don't wanna remember.

DELROY. Fuck you. He gonna bring money for a quarter key, tonight. You be there, and you make some money.

DWIGHT. You got a quarter, B?

DELROY. He think I got a quarter. He gonna bring money for a quarter.

DWIGHT. Word. My ass so broke, 'bout to rob Baskin Robbins.

DELROY. Y'get a third watchin my back. Now, listen up to my shit. Arright?! I know y'ass got nothin' else to do. Here it go, mom, this it…

(Music.)

(straight to Dwight.)

My dick bust the ground.

My nuts hang n' clang.

I'm the killa on the mike you wanna shotta to bang.

DWIGHT. … ohhhhh!

DELROY. My ride's a Benz so fine it make the bitches get wet.

They slide off the seat when they climb inside to ride to my video set.

DWIGHT. Oh!

DELROY. Y'show y'ho a subway ride

y'grab her bony booty in the middle of the car

y'want everybody know

she y'skinny white ho

slide her hand to y'dick

make the whole train sick

see y'tongue-kiss

Baskin Robbin lips

That drips 31 flavors a cum

she suck from cock

like a straw in a shake

To get a 3 dollar rock

y'think y'it

y'the it in idiot

y'don't even know

y'the idiot show

    on the Bronx bound number one
    on y'way to do a video –
    for Koolio!

DWIGHT. …killa!

DELROY. y'shits cheap!
    my nuts swing
    they hang n'clang
    the killa on the mike y'wanna shotta to bang

DWIGHT. Killa Crisis!!

DELROY. my crunch make the bitches cling
    y'nothin, y'frontin,
    y'the zero in the middle of my cheerio!

DWIGHT. Crisis in the house!

DELROY. Killa Crisis!

DWIGHT. Killa! …ohhhhhh!

(They do a "chest bump")

DWIGHT. *(continued)* Tonight.

DELROY. Tonight. Nine on time.

(Music up, loud, out.)

Scene 6

(Front room. **LENA** *and* **IRENE.***)*

IRENE. A crack head. Great.

LENA. What was I suppose to say?

IRENE. How bout you don't want him here.

LENA. They were in the army together. Danny wants to do the right thing.

IRENE. He's on something. He slept all day.

LENA. D says he's clean.

IRENE. He probably did some weak ten day rehab.

LENA. Three months, D said, in the VA.

IRENE. It's your shit, but D's wrong to bring him here.

(They hear a thump. A muted reaction. **RAY,** *enters.)*

RAY. Sorry to bother you. What's the address?

LENA. 421. 175th.

*(***RAY** *exits, rear.)*

IRENE. I'm gonna call D.

LENA. He's not picking up. He's like he gets when he's into something. He said just another day at work like he does when it's not.

RAY. *(returns)* What apartment?

LENA. 5.

*(***RAY** *exits, rear.)*

IRENE. I'll leave a message. He's gotta tell this two dollar pebble head to go.

(Speed dials. She holds phone from ear. Johnny Cash song, I've Been Everywhere: "Panama Mattua LaPaloma Bangor –" Daniel's voice: 'this is Danny, leave a message' – "Amarillo Tocapillo Pocotello –" BEEP.)

This is Irene. Call-me-back. Unless your cell don't work on Brokeback Mountain.

RAY. *(returns)* There's a nurse gonna come to see me.

LENA. What happen'd?

RAY. Danny said it'd be Ok she comes.

LENA. A nurse?

RAY. Yeah. From the VA.

IRENE. I'm Daniel's sister.

RAY. Oh. Yeah.

IRENE. What's your name?

RAY. Ray.

IRENE. This is Daniel's wife. This is her apartment you're in.

RAY. Uh-huh. I appreciate what y'do. I don't want to be no burden. I'm getting it together…get work, get a room…anyway, she's comin' by, so, she's on her way, so, probably mosts bout fifteen minutes.

(**RAY** *goes back.*)

LENA. He look like a hero to you?

IRENE. A hero?

LENA. He ran out into all kinds of bullets to save people.

IRENE. That mess did?

LENA. Then he went back again for Gulf 2, or whatever they call it.

IRENE. How crazy is that?

LENA. The towers made people patriotic.

IRENE. D's patriotic. But he didn't get crazy and go back.

LENA. He met me.

IRENE. Crazy got him anyway.

LENA. Yrright.

IRENE. He didn't have to go to a foreign country *twice.*

LENA. Uh-uh, no.

IRENE. Enough crazy shit right here.

LENA. Yrright.

IRENE. It caught me at my laundromat. A woman came at me cuz I wouldn't back off the jumbo machine holds four loads for four-fifty. She acted like she didn't have the only other jumbo going already. She asked me how many machines do I need? I only had a little dollar fifty one running with whites.

LENA. Drop it off at Bubbles for fluff 'n' fold. Let them do it for you.

IRENE. I'm too cheap.

LENA. It's worth the money not to get messed with by bitches over machines.

IRENE. She wore a T said "Got milk?" across giant bazookas.

LENA. "Got milk?"

IRENE. Shit didn't hide her belly. She kept stretching it down like she's gonna make it fit, talking like it's gonna get messy unless I back off it. I had a full gallon size of Xtra concentrated ready to hit her in the head and knock her ass out.

LENA. Holy shit.

(**IRENE**'s *cell rings.* **RAY** *appears unseen to the women during the phone call.*)

IRENE. *(answering)* What is wrong with you inviting this loser to move in? Then why's a crack head here? No, you! No, you! You! Cowboy asshole!

(disconnects)

He's wound up.

RAY. Excuse me, sorry, there a towel I should use?

LENA. *(exiting)* Yeah, hang on.

RAY. I pick up after myself.

IRENE. Why shouldn't you?

RAY. I do in case y'think I don't.

IRENE. Don't think you can game anyone here.

RAY. Uh-uh, no way, that's not the real me.

IRENE. I'm not talking about the real you. I'm taking about crackheaded you.

LENA. *(entering, towel)* You was in Iraq with Danny?

RAY. Yeah, '91. Pretty much.

LENA. You went back for Gulf 2 or whatever it was called?

RAY. Endearin' Freedom. Arright, well…thanks.

(He exits.)

IRENE. He's a crack head. Don't get feeling sorry for his ass.

LENA. Don't worry.

IRENE. Don't forget what happened to me.

LENA. Irene?

IRENE. What? I'm just telling it like it is. Sylvia's daddy had me feeling sorry for him right up to the last time he went into emergency and didn't come out.

(Buzzer. **LENA** *goes to the intercom.)*

LENA. Who is it?

MARA. *(V.O.)* Mara.

LENA. Who?

MARA. *(V.O.)* Is Ray there?

IRENE. Ask is she the nurse.

LENA. You from the VA?

MARA. *(V.O.)* Yes. From VA.

(She buzzes **MARA** *into the building.)*

IRENE. Sounds like my super from Kosovo.

LENA. Wha'happened?

IRENE. The country was bombed all to shit?

LENA. I forgot already. I learned all the names when I met Danny. He was into it. Ko-so-vo. Her-ze-go-vi-na. Sa-ra-je-vo. To impress him. Stupid, huh?

(Bell rings. She lets in **MARA.** *Short skirt. Boots. Jewelry.)*

MARA. Hello.

LENA. I'm Lena. This is Irene.

IRENE. You're a nurse?

MARA. Yes.

LENA. You want something to drink? Water…soda…?

MARA. Beer?

LENA. Yeah. Irene?

IRENE. No.

LENA. Glass of beer coming up.

   (exiting)

IRENE. Hey! Hey! The nurse is here! What, you brought him medication?

MARA. Pardon?

IRENE. Med-i-ca-tion?

MARA. I can't talk about patients because of patient privacy rule.

IRENE. Are you here as his nurse?

MARA. Friend.

IRENE. Where are you from?

MARA. Russia.

IRENE. You're allowed to speak freely in this country.

MARA. I'm a U.S. Citizen.

IRENE. Then you know the First Amendment.

MARA. Russia, you talk about treatment, no problem, but VA has patient privacy rule.

IRENE. Your friend, Ray, is here because his friend, Daniel, who is my brother, and her husband, wants to help him. I want to know if under the crack head, there lives a psychotic war monster, and if you have to make sure he takes his meds, so that the monster doesn't come out and kill everyone here.

MARA. Nothing. No.

   *(**LENA** enters with a glass of beer. **MARA** drinks it down.)*

   Thirsty. Perfect. Thank you.

   *(**RAY** enters. New shirt and pants.)*

   Very nice clothes.

RAY. My friend got 'em for me.

MARA. You look better.

RAY. We're goin' for a drink. Maybe catch a movie.

MARA. Nice to meet you.

LENA. You, too.

RAY. Anyone care to join us?

LENA. We've work to do.

RAY. Danny gave me keys, so…

(They exit.)

IRENE. I bite my tongue.

LENA. I have worksheets to make. You wanna grade your papers now or after we smoke up?

*(**IRENE** takes student school work from a satchel.)*

IRENE. Maybe while we smoke.

*(**LENA** hits music player as she exits to get her student's work.)*

Get my head right. Let me read you this from the 9th grader I got into it with about the "nigga" thing.

*(**LENA** returns with folder of worksheets, homework to grade, etc.)*

LENA. Nigga is *the* word, isn't it?

IRENE. I told her it's not about not saying "nigga." I said, that maybe of all the words there are, "nigga" is not the best one to describe Bambi.

LENA. They showed Bambi?

IRENE. In home room.

LENA. Stupid.

*(**LENA** rolls up a smoke as they talk. Eventually lights it and passes it to **IRENE**.)*

IRENE. I asked the class how they felt about Bambi losing his mother. My girl said, "Why care what happened to the lil nigga? He's a cartoon."

*(There's a beat before they burst into laughter. **IRENE** opens a folder of her students work, and retrieves a letter and a Lil Kim CD.)*

This is why I love her. She brought in a story from the newspaper about they sent Lil Kim to some cold ass prison in Philadelphia for lying, and why did lying white Martha Stewart get to go to some soft prison nicknamed cup cake. They all said it was bullshit. So, I thought I'd take advantage of it. I'd bring in some Lil Kim to play, and have them write to Lil Kim in jail. Tell Lil Kim about their life. Get them expressing it. You heard Lil Kim?

LENA. I know who she is.

IRENE. Listen to this. And they know this, y'know, my kids, they know all this by heart.

(She plays "How Many Licks." They pass the J. Smoke. The song plays through the intro.)

LENA. You played it?

IRENE. No way!

LENA. Your ass would be so fired.

IRENE. So fired.

LENA. It's so not appropriate.

IRENE. It's so dirty.

(They listen. Irene turns it down.)

IRENE. *(continued)* I said write to Lil Kim. Show her some love. This is what my girl wrote.

(reads:)

My name is Ejona. I live in Apartment 34, in Harlem, in New York. My friend Daryl Moore was shot dead on our block. His school photograph is on a cardboard hung on the rail in front of the building. There are ribbons and flowers, and a silver heart balloon. They wrote R.I.P. You at rest now. I love you. R.I.P. I'll miss you. R.I.P. See you in heaven, peace, my lil nephew, is what his uncle A-rab wrote. Nineteen lit candles and nineteen empty bottles of brandy and a 40 with red bandanas tied around for pride on the sidewalk where he died. The whole block cried the day my friend Daryl Moore got shot and died."

(Music.)

Scene 7

*(Empty lot. Night. **DELROY** and **DWIGHT** share hits of crack.)*

DWIGHT. I thought y'put this shit down.

DELROY. I did, but I dinnit forget where it wuz put.

DWIGHT. I hear that.

DELROY. They the Prada ODB y'got on, my nigga?

DWIGHT. Uh-huh. Y'all notice?

DELROY. They the limited?

DWIGHT. Limited edition. ODB, R.I.P. Pradas.

DELROY. They ain't suppose to be out yet.

DWIGHT. They ain't out.

DELROY. They on your feet.

DWIGHT. I got 'em advanced at the Hot Dot down by McDonalds.

DELROY. I'm gonna get the green tops. Wear with my Jets fitted.

DWIGHT. Y'might get em down there.

DELROY. I heard y'the first time, nigga.

DWIGHT. Y'hear "I gotta take y'myself to meet my cousin works at Hot Dot or y'won't get shit because they ain't even suppose to have 'em?" You hear that, nigga?

DELROY. I hear it now, nigga.

DWIGHT. Uh-huh. Where's the nigga gonna give us some money, B?

DELROY. He deserve gettin' licked. Like I don't gotta be somewhere else.

DWIGHT. The nigga got it, we gonna get it.

DELROY. He gonna have it.

DWIGHT. Too bad we got nothin to play him, so he go deep, B.

DELROY. How we supposed to play him?

DWIGHT. If we had sump'n.

DELROY. Nigga, we gettin sump'n for nuth'n.

DWIGHT. If we did, I'm sayin', *If* –

DELROY. Fuck ifs nigga –

DWIGHT. – you ain't listened!

DELROY. You ain't sayin nothin!

DWIGHT. I'm sayin' *if* we could…*if*, B, *if* we could get some pure coke! We could bait the greedy money muthafuken nigga he got. Get him deep in his pocket.

DELROY. Where we get pure cocaine to bait the muthafuka?

DWIGHT. Those M.O. bitches you know.

DELROY. They crazy ass niggas. Know what I'm sayin? They wanna take the money they self they learn what we do. Know what I'm sayin? The nigga Big Elephant stay over General Grant projects got licked by some crazy MOBville nigga'n he son of Scarface! He so mad he shot some nigga right on 151, 'n the nigga he shot a MOBville mascot nigga. That's when y'was already in jail or was hiding from police up y'boys in Buffalo. Big Elephant told the muthafuka get in the jeep to go someplace away from the block to talk. Lil nigga said no. Elephant shot his ass right there. He wuz jis a little dime haze nigga. But he fuck with Elephant. Y'fuck Big Elephant, you gonna be 187.

DWIGHT. Where Elephant been at?

DELROY. He ain't dead yet, or in jail, then he probably down DC with his grams, or some shit. Where is this bitch? Tip off in thirty minutes.

DWIGHT. Who y'take?

DELROY. Phoenix, who y'think I got?

DWIGHT. Ten it Detroit.

DELROY. Phoenix got Jamal. He gonna squash it in Wallace face.

DWIGHT. Jamal a high school nigga gonna meet a grown man at the rim, n' he choke like a bitch!

DELROY. Then double up, nigga.

DWIGHT. Y'on. That y'nigga comin?

DELROY. That's him.

(**DWIGHT** *produces a 22 caliber gun.*)

What y'gonna do with y'little lady gun?

DWIGHT. It do what gotta get done.

DELROY. Don't make it more than it is, cuz.

DWIGHT. Nigga look familiar.

DELROY. Y'know the nigga?

DWIGHT. He look familiar.

DELROY. Stay back a minute.

(**DWIGHT** *steps back.* **DELROY** *steps forward to meet* **DANIEL**.)

DANIEL. Where my shit? It 100 percent, he gonna owe me a mad IOU. Cuz my bank wants the boat load.

DELROY. You got the money?

(**DWIGHT** *steps forward.*)

He's my cousin.

DANIEL. *(nods)* What up?

DWIGHT. I know you, nigga.

DANIEL. I don't know you. Here's the money, Delroy.

(**DANIEL** *puts his hand in a black plastic deli bag.*)

DWIGHT. You a narc muthafuka.

(*They fire simultaneously.* **DANIEL** *fires from the gun concealed in the bag. Both fall.* **DELROY** *is frozen for a moment. Looks at* **DWIGHT**'s *motionless body. Music.*)

DELROY. Mother fuck. Dwight? Ah…Dwight. Mother fuck.

(*He suddenly has to urinate.*)

Shit, shit, shit.

(*pissing*)

Ah, fuck, yeah…ah… .

(*looking at* **DANIEL**)

I *owe* you, muthafuka? I OWE YOU? Here my IOU.

(*He urinates on* **DANIEL**. *Music.*)

Scene 8

(Front room. **LENA** *and* **IRENE** *look at finger paintings.* **LENA** *finds one she's looking for.)*

LENA. She loves to make things. She's happy when she is. This is her drawing.

IRENE. You think she saw it happened?

LENA. I think so. She was 2. She sat by her mother all night.

IRENE. Fucking awful…her mother's boyfriend?

LENA. Yeah…I don't know where she put it in her, somewhere, but…you wouldn't know, y'know, she's really sweet.

IRENE. *(starts getting her stuff together)* I gotta pick up Lil Sylvia.

LENA. Arright.

IRENE. I can't wait around any longer to set my brother's ass straight. Lil Sylvia, Lil Kim, lil Bambi. It's catchy.

LENA. Give her a kiss from lil' Auntie.

(sound of buzzer)

Shit, who's this?

IRENE. Crackheaded Ray probably lost his keys already.

LENA. *(uses intercom)* Who is it?

DETECTIVE MONROE. *(V.O)* Mrs. Prats?

LENA. Who is this?

DETECTIVE MONROE. *(V.O)* I'm Detective Monroe. I'd like to come up and talk to you.

LENA. Why?

DETECTIVE MONROE. *(V.O)* Please, I'd like to come up. Mrs. Prats?

LENA. Is it about my husband?

DETECTIVE MONROE. *(V.O)* I'd like to talk to you.

LENA. Is it Danny?

DETECTIVE MONROE. *(V.O.)* Let me up, please, Mrs. Prats.

IRENE. We should let him in.

LENA. Where's my phone? Something happened.

IRENE. *(buzzing Monroe up)* You don't know.

LENA. Why's he here? I gotta call Danny. Something happened.

IRENE. You don't know... !

LENA. Why's he here? Something bad...

(She finds her mobile. She can barely breathe. Makes the call. Immobile as she listens to message. Knock on door. She drops the phone. Lena goes to the door and opens it.)

DETECTIVE MONROE. *(showing ID badge)* Detective Monroe. May I come in?

Scene 9

*(Music. Front room. **RAY** and **MARA** enter. He stands blurry eyed, keeping his balance. He searches pockets for a cigarette.)*

RAY. Come to my room.

MARA. I don't want to.

RAY. You don't wanna?

MARA. I'm going.

RAY. Wait a minute.

(He attempts to seduce her into it.)

MARA. They'll wake up.

(He ends up on the floor.)

I told you don't mix with Klonopin. Call me.

(She exits. He tries to get up, fails.)

RAY. Danny. Danny. I can't get up. Come out and talk to me. I'm gonna crawl then. Crawlin' to see my friend. I fucked up! Someone is gonna be mad.

(realizes no one's home)

Fuck.

*(sees **LENA**'s phone searches menu)*

A-B-C. D. Danny.

*(He calls **DANIEL**. He starts to talk, stops when he realizes it's the message, and waits for it to end.)*

Hey, cowboy. I jis want t'say thank you. Thank you. I don't know where y'are. No one's here…but me. But… thank you, man…Thank you…

(He exits. Music.)

Scene 10

(Front room. **LENA, IRENE,** *and* **RAY** *are seated.* **DETECTIVE MONROE***–suit, tie)*

DETECTIVE MONROE. The PBA, the department, everyone is in your corner.

LENA. Thank you.

DETECTIVE MONROE. Special Services contacted you?

LENA. Yes.

DETECTIVE MONROE. Good. They make arrangements for the bed, safety rails in tbe bathroom, whatever's needed. They'll make sure it's done.

LENA. Thank you.

DETECTIVE MONROE. I understand you work, a teacher?

LENA. I'm on temporary leave.

DETECTIVE MONROE. You'll need help when Danny comes home.

RAY. I'm gonna be helpin.

DETECTIVE MONROE. A day nurse is covered for a limited time.

LENA. 6 weeks.

DETECTIVE MONROE. There's a medical van avail for transport to and from therapy. I think it's Columbia Presbyterian?

LENA. Yes.

DETECTIVE MONROE. OK. So…um…Is there anything you've remembered? It may not seem important to you, but anything, no matter how small, y'know, name of a bar, the name of a street…

RAY. He shot the man dead. They something else?

DETECTIVE MONROE. You knew Detective Prats from serving together in Iraq?

RAY. Yeah.

DETECTIVE MONROE. He visited you in the V.A?

RAY. Yeah.

DETECTIVE MONROE. Nothing was mentioned about what he was doing?

RAY. I don't much remember from then. Those days were –

DETECTIVE MONROE. *(cuts him off)* We need you, where can I find you?

RAY. Y'can find me here.

DETECTIVE MONROE. You're staying here?

RAY. I'm here to help Danny.

DETECTIVE MONROE. OK. The doctor said another week he'll come home.

LENA. Yes.

IRENE. *(confused by this)* No, no. They have to operate again.

LENA. They don't think they should.

IRENE. They have to get the rest of the bullet.

LENA. They decided it's safer not to.

IRENE. Who decided?

RAY. Maybe if there's nothin else.

DETECTIVE MONROE. *(annoyed)* Excuse me?

RAY. Considerin. Y'know? People upset?

DETECTIVE MONROE. Everyone's upset. A cop was shot.

> *(to **LENA**)*
>
> I wanted to see that everything was taken care of, seeing he's coming home, and tell you Danny is in everyone's prayers.

LENA. Thank you.

DETECTIVE MONROE. Don't hesitate to call. Detective Monroe. Anytime.

> *(The **DETECTIVE** leaves.)*

IRENE. Danny has family to take care of him.

RAY. I want to help.

IRENE. You're gonna stay off crack?

RAY. It's been 4 months.

LENA. Irene. Danny's three-fourths won't cover everything as it is. You work, and have to take care of a daughter.

I'll have to go back to work. We need all the help we can get.

RAY. Nurse Mara's gonna help. I'm gonna get a job. I'm gonna work and help take care of Danny. Doctor said I was good, didn't he?

LENA. Yes.

RAY. Tell her what he said.

LENA. He said Danny responded well to Ray. He said he was really good with him.

IRENE. You're making all the decisions about Danny?

LENA. He's my husband.

IRENE. When was it decided not to operate.

LENA. Yesterday.

IRENE. You didn't talk to me about it.

LENA. I'm sorry.

IRENE. Did you know?

RAY. No.

LENA. They decided it was better not to. It could make it worse. He could die. I want him home. He needs to learn everything again. To talk. To understand. To remember...

(Her emotions stop her. **IRENE** *holds her.)*

IRENE. I'm sorry. I love you. I'm sorry.

LENA. I know. I love you. I need you. You'll be late. You better go pick up Sylvia.

IRENE. I'll take her to her grandmother, and come back.

LENA. No. I'm OK. I'll toughen up. Call me.

IRENE. *(to* **RAY***)* Believe me. I know about crack, so, y'know, first sign...

(to **LENA***)*

I'll call.

*(***IRENE** *exits.)*

RAY. Danny don't give up. Hell broke open in the desert. He didn't move back. He stayed. He don't give up. *(Music. "comin home.")*

Scene 11

(Front room. RAY's hanging a "Welcome Home" decoration across a wall. Helium filled heart balloons are tied to a new easy chair. The mobile on the table rings.)

RAY. *(continued)* Y'phone. Y'phone. Y'phone!

(IRENE bustles in from the kitchen with a vase with flowers.)

IRENE. Hello. OK.

(to RAY)

They're here. They took a cab. You should go down.

RAY. No medical van "avail" like Detective Asshole said. Like they said about a lot of shit.

IRENE. Go already!

(He exits. Buzzer. IRENE answers intercom.)

Lena?

LENA. *(V.O.)* Yeah.

(IRENE buzzes her in. Unlocks door. She puts Johnny Cash CD in player. She cues and plays "I've Been Everywhere." She does last minute needless adjustment to room.)

LENA. *(continued) (entering)* They said don't make too much of his home coming.

IRENE. We should take Welcome Home down?

LENA. Maybe. I don't know. I better go help.

(She exits. IRENE quickly takes the sign down. Exits. She returns, hurries to untie the balloons and pick up the vase of flowers. She starts to exit but stops at the sound of RAY, Daniel, LENA.)

RAY *(offstage)* OK, Danny, y'got it. No, this way, yeah…

(Lena enters. DANIEL enters. RAY is close behind. DANIEL's head is bandaged. He makes involuntary facial tics. Nothing's familiar to him. He's unsure of spacial relationships. "I've Been Everywhere" plays on.)

ACT TWO

Scene 12

(Loading dock. Night. **DELROY** *sucks a crack pipe. He thinks he hears someone.)*

DELROY. Who that?

(looks, listens)

Who there? Dwight?
148th. Shit.

(hits pipe)

People know me. Know who I am. Get my Spanky beats.

(Puts on headphones. Improvises a few beats. Removes headphones. Hits pipe, feels effect.) Yeah, shit. Oh Oh Oh Oh... Ain't no rap. Story of me. Killa Crisis. Harlem nigga. Primary School 153. Teacher said I'm nothin! Never be somethin! Can't bother with me. I said, suck my dick, y' ain't shit to me! Y'ain't nothin!

CROWD. *(V.O.)* Ain't nothin.

(Puts on headphones. He imagines the crowd and the beats that are heard.)

DELROY. 10 years old tryin to make it on an uptown free. Transit Cop has to hassle me. Say he Abe Lincoln, if I beg, he gonna set me free, laughin at me. I said, suck my dick, y'ain't shit to me! He put a beatin on me. Ain't nothin!

DELROY/CROWD. *(V.O.)* Ain't nothin!

DELROY. Beatin ain't nothin!

DELROY/CROWD. *(V.O.)* Ain't nothin!

(Takes off headphones. Takes hit. Leaves headphones off.)

DELROY. I'm Killa Crisis outta project houses. Projects ain't nothin!

DELROY/CROWD. *(V.O.)* Ain't nothin.

DELROY. Got names to sound like they something.

DELROY/CROWD. *(V.O.)* Ain't nothin.

DELROY. Harborview Terrace.

DELROY/CROWD. *(V.O.)* Ain't nothin.

DELROY. Polo Grounds Houses.

DELROY/CROWD. *(V.O.)* Ain't nothin.

DELROY. Manhattanville Homes.

DELROY/CROWD. *(V.O.)* Ain't nothin.

DELROY. Projects, seen a few, son, worked rock in one or two, son. I've seen La Guardia Homes, Harlem River Homes, Strauss Houses, Wagner Houses, Thurgood Marshall Plaza, Campos Plaza, a disaster – seen Holmes Towers, Dewitt Towers Two Bridges, Ira Robbins, Gompers, Audubon Bethune, J Weldon Johnson, Frawly, Lehman, see what I mean, the fucken projects I've seen? George Washington Carver Houses, sold some green in Gaylord Flower Towers, another fucken precedent, moved crack in projects named for presidents, Wilson, Washington, Grant, Lincoln, Taft – what a laugh! Projects seen a few, son, moved some D in one or two, son. I've been to St. Nics, Douglass, Randolph, Hamilton, Raphael Hernendez, Wise Towers, Rutger Homes, Jacob Riis, all the nigga reservations, all the house consolidations, Jackie Robinson Consolidation, Metro North Consolidation, Lower East Side I & II Consolidations, can't forget Amsterdam, Baruch, Fulton, Viadeck, Grampton, Rengal. Frederick, Meltzer, Seeward Park, Crampton Villa, I'm a killa. Projects where I come from, every fuckin one, son, joined a set in one, son, every fuckin one, son, learn the colors then, son, every fuckin one, son, red is for my blood, son, green is for the money, son, brown's the dirt I come from, I only trust me, son, talk come from a gun, son, it talks, y'shit's done, son! Oh oh oh- ohhhh! Oh oh oh- ohhhh!

(Crowd echoes him: "Oh oh oh." Music.)

Scene 13

(Front room. **DANIEL***'s finger painting.* **RAY***'s picking up other paintings.)*

RAY. Y'gettin' better at doin things. Soon y'wipe y'own ass. Arright, finger paintin over. Time to clean up. Let's see what y'got. This a tree? You make a tree? I'll just file this with the others.

*(***RAY*** exits.* **DANIEL** *tries to name part a word that he sees in his head.)*

DANIEL. Gra. Gra...gra. ga...

*(***RAY*** returns with soft wipes to clean paint off* **DANIEL***)*

RAY. Try'n see the whole word, the doctor said. Y'forget the first part of the word when y'look for the second part of the word. If y'see "tree," I'm not sayin y'do, but if y'see tree in y'mind, don't get hung up on the "tr" part and be askin yourself what is that? What's that? "Trr" What's that tr.tr.trrr... and the ee part is gone. It goes cuz of not keepin the whole word in y'mind. "Trrreeee."

(Buzzer. He buzzes downstairs, then unlocks the door.)

Nurse Mara's here to give me a break from y'ass. I'm gonna get us some chicken. Some beans and rice. Some plantains. Some oxtails. Some avocado salad. What y'feel?

DANIEL. ...gra...

RAY. Let it out whatever it is. See the whole word.

DANIEL. Grape...

RAY. Say, what... ?

DANIEL. *(to himself)* Grape...grape...

RAY. He said words start to come, they come like a muthafuka, n' don't worry they don't make no sense, just flow.

*(***DETECTIVE MONROE*** enters. Knocks on inside of door.* **RAY** *turns expecting* **MARA***.)*

DETECTIVE MONROE. You look disappointed?

RAY. Y'ain't the nurse s'all.

DETECTIVE MONROE. Teach you to ask who it is before letting people up.

(to **DANIEL***)*

Detective Monroe – from the 3-0. Think he remembers me?

RAY. Maybe.

DETECTIVE MONROE. He understand what you say?

RAY. Maybe. Talk slow.

DETECTIVE MONROE. I-came-by-to-ask-about-the-other-prick-was-there.

DANIEL. *(quietly to himself)* Sla…sla…

RAY. They someone else?

DETECTIVE MONROE. What?

RAY. They someone else?

DETECTIVE MONROE. What's with the breakdown of language?

RAY. What?

DETECTIVE MONROE. The breakdown of human language.

RAY. He's findin words.

DETECTIVE MONROE. I'm talking about you. "They someone else?"

RAY. Was they?

DETECTIVE MONROE. "They someone else" doesn't make sense.

RAY. Don't it?

DETECTIVE MONROE. What do you mean, "finding words?"

RAY. Where he shot the "Wernicke's area." Where language at. That's how the doctor explained it. Someone say somethin' important, I hear it. That's why I ax'd you "They someone else?"

DETECTIVE MONROE. "Ax'd" me?

RAY. Yeah.

DETECTIVE MONROE. I don't speak ebonics.

DANIEL. *(neutral voice)* Round smoke day rain dollar run cat cloud shoe ball clock war tide corn swing grass black rock rat can red bench bird hat steel flag salt.

(DANIEL gets up and moves about agitatedly. RAY reaches for DANIEL's hand.)

RAY. He about to shit. Come on.

(buzzer)

That be Mara.

DETECTIVE MONROE. You better hurry.

(RAY and DANIEL exit.)

DETECTIVE MONROE. *(continued)* Jesus, that his stink?

RAY. *(off)* Buzz the woman up.

(DETECTIVE MONROE talks into intercom)

Who is it?

MARA. *(V.O) (intercom)* Mara. Who are you?

DETECTIVE MONROE. Detective Monroe.

(DETECTIVE MONROE buzzes the downstairs. Listens to RAY, who is off stage.)

RAY *(offstage to Danny)* Let's get your pants off. Don't worry about a little shit. It don't matter. y'human's all. Everyone craps. Maybe not their pants so much…now y' drawers… .

(DETECTIVE MONROE steps out into the hall.)

DETECTIVE MONROE. *(to MARA, who is off)* Talk to you a minute.

(He shuts the door.)

(Music.)

Scene 14

(Front room. **RAY** *wears a security guard uniform.* **DANIEL** *walks back and forth in a caged gate.)*

DANIEL. K-L-B-N

RAY. 0...Come on, man, yr'doin' great.

DANIEL. Bored.

RAY. What'dya say?

*(**RAY** wears a security guard uniform.)*

DANIEL. Bored. Alphabet. Boring.

RAY. What?

DANIEL. Boring.

RAY. Fuck me...Y'makin sense?

(after a moment)

When y'was shot? They someone else? Cuz y'raise the name, I'll find 'em. I'll kill him.

LENA. *(entering)* I'm late.

RAY. No problem.

LENA. I had to wait with a kid for his dad.

RAY. Danny spoke about somethin' was "related," like the therapist said, y'know? He said he was bored with the alphabet.

DANIEL. Bored.

LENA. Bored, Danny? That true?

DANIEL. Alphabet. Bor-ing.

LENA. *(hugs him)* Boring. Yeah. Good. That's great.

(gratefully)

Oh, is that great.

RAY. Arright. I gotta go be bored at this dumb ass job I'm grateful I got.

LENA. Good luck.

RAY. Arright.

DANIEL. Arright.

(He exits. She caresses **DANIEL***.)*

LENA. I love you. You know that, right? I love you?

(He's confused. He moves away.)

Danny.

DANIEL. *(neutral)* Danny. Lena.

LENA. That's my name, but...

(slower)

You need anything?

(He shakes his head.)

I'm going to change.

(She exits. He searches for a memory - feeling - to put with the name but none surfaces.)

DANIEL. *(quietly)* ...Lena...?

(Music.)

Scene 15

*(Loading dock. **DELROY** fires a torch lighter and sucks on crack pipe. Attempts to play disc player. It doesn't work.)*

DELROY. Shit.

(Slaps it.)

Bitch.

(It doesn't work.)

Man...

(Unplugs earphones. Takes out "beats" disc.)

Get me a Sony.

(Beats disc man with bat. Tosses it away. Ties beats disc on end of earphone line.)

...spanky...

(Hits pipe. Music.)

who the gansta
who do gansta things
homey Dwight in dead gansta heaven
got a gold plated Glock
given him by other dead
nigga angels in dead
gansta heaven got shot
Crips, Bloods, Qaeda niggas
all live in dead gansta nigga heaven on the same block
so shootin don't stop

y'don't die ya shot
y'always dyin
y'always shot
y'capped by a gat
y'don't die
y'chopped by a mac
y'don't die

y'shot round the clock in dead nigga gansta angel heaven
shootin don't stop
y'don't die ya shot
y'always dyin
y'always shot
y'dyin don't stop
y'always dyin
y'always shot

Scene 16

*(Front room. **DANIEL** asleep in the chair. A new TV is on a trolly. Daytime soap plays. In small rear room, **RAY** and **MARA** having sex.)*

MARA *(offstage) (moans to yells)* Da. Da. Oh. Ahhhh! Jebat'-kopat'! Oh Ray. You fucking me? You fucking me? Vstat' rakom. Da! Ah! Oh. Ray. Ahhhh. God. Oh. Yobar' Ahhhh Da!

RAY *(offstage)* Not so loud.

*(**DANIEL** wakes, confused. He exits in their direction.)*

MARA *(offstage)* Ahhhhh. Khuj. Fuck me. Fuck me. Yobar'! Yobar'! Da! Da! Da. Da. Trakhat'Jebat'-kopat'! Jebat'-kopat'! Yobar' Yobar' Da…Da…Ah!

(pause)

Danny!

*(**DANIEL** enters, agitated. **RAY** enters tying up sweats.)*

RAY. Danny. Hey, it's OK.

*(**MARA** enters, unzipped, unbuttoned.)*

MARA. Danny. Don't be upset. It's OK.

RAY. Yeah, man, we like each other's all. I'm sorry, man, y'were asleep, man, so we got together.

MARA. Don't be upset. Let me hug you.

RAY. Yeah, man, shit, it looked weird, I know, but we were ballin' is all. It's called ballin'.

DANIEL. "Ballin."

RAY. Yeah, man, ballin'. That's it.

(hugs him)

Let me give y'some love, man.

*(to **MARA**)*

It had to be weird. Hear Russian screamed out.

MARA. *(to **DANIEL**)* Sit down. I'll make some tea. OK. Get words. I'll put on water.

*(to **RAY**)*

Turn off the shit TV.

*(She exits. **RAY** turns off TV. He fetches picture-word cards. **DANIEL** turns on the TV.)*

(offstage) Ray, turn off shit TV!

RAY. She's right, Danny, let's turn it off.

*(**RAY** turns it off. **DANIEL** turns the TV back on.)*

Come on, don't be like that.

*(**RAY** turns it off. **DANIEL** kicks it.)*

That's a brand new fuckin' TV, man! Don't hit the TV! Shit cost money!

MARA. *(entering)* Don't be asshole cuz fuck was cut short. I'll do words with Danny. Don't mind him. He's being asshole. Two new words.

(holds up card)

A new picture. OK.

DANIEL. That's a…What? It's… a… I don't know… Round… Round… Ba…ba…

MARA. Bi-cy-cle.

DANIEL. *(accent)* Bi-cy-cle.

RAY. It's not Russian.

MARA. Shut up.

*(**MARA** holds up new card. **RAY** struggles to decipher it.)*

Tick tock…tick tock.

RAY. Give the man time, shit.

MARA. CCClooock.

RAY. Clock.

MARA. That's what I said.

RAY. In fuckin' Russian.

DANIEL. *(accent)* CCClooock.

RAY. Jesus. I'm goin' for a walk.

MARA. Good.

RAY. *(to* **DANIEL***)* Don't become communist while I'm gone.

*(***RAY** *exits.)*

MARA. Khuilo. *(to* **DANIEL***)* Bicycle. Clock.

MARA/DANIEL. Bicycle. Clock.

*(***MARA** *holds up another card.)*

MARA. Alphabet.

DANIEL. E.Z.

MARA. Backwards.

DANIEL. Z Y X W V U T S R Q P O N M L K...um...

(louder)

J I H G F E D C B A E Z

(Tea kettle whistles.)

MARA. I'll make tea. Then we will practise vowels. Remember vowel sounds?

DANIEL. *(exaggerates sound)* VOW-ELS.

MARA. *(exiting)* A.E.I.O.U...

DANIEL. *(introspectively)* ... I.O.U? IOU?

(Music.)

Scene 17

(Front room. **LENA**, **IRENE**. **DANIEL** *has a big serving of mashed potatoes. TV heard in rear.)*

LENA. Only Danny knew how to get the old one to work. I came home, Ray had bought a new TV. He brings it out when I'm not here. So Danny can learn from it, he says. I understand, but y'know how that goes. I don't want it to end up out here 24/7.

*(***DANIEL*** gets a big spoon of mashed potato to his mouth.)*

Good, D, baby.

(TV is turned off in rear. **RAY** *enters in his security guard uniform.)*

RAY. We're gonna start readin'a book Mara pickin up. Ghetto Cop # 1. They 25 of them. So, y'like it. We get #2. Y' like 2, we get Ghetto Cop #3, on up, 4, 5, so on.

(He starts out. **DANIEL**, *eating, picks up the count as the scene goes on. At 25, he starts backwards.)*

DANIEL. *(neutral voice)* …6…7…8…

RAY. Mara be by 8 o'clock. See y'all.

LENA. OK.

IRENE. Be safe.

RAY. *(exiting)* Y'warmin' to me. But y'too late.

IRENE. *(to* **LENA***)* You know what? Mara gets here, come with me to pick up the kid. We'll stop in the lounge over there and have a drink.

*(***DANIEL*** loads his plate with more potatoes.)*

DANIEL. 14…15…16…

IRENE. Give the Hide-A-Way "Happy Hour" crowd reason to hope.

LENA. Maybe you'll get lucky.

IRENE. I'm lucky when I want.

LENA. Someone I don't know about?

DANIEL. 22…23…

IRENE. Mmm…No.

(DANIEL lifts a small mountain of potatoes toward his mouth. He stops mid-air, looking intently at the spoon full of mashed potatoes.)

My God.

LENA. What you gonna do with all that?

DANIEL. Eat.

(swallows)

24…25…25…24…

IRENE. What about you and Danny? Is it going on yet?

LENA. No…

IRENE. He's OK there? I mean…?

LENA. I don't know if we should talk about it.

IRENE. Talk fast so he can't understand.

LENA. *(slowly, to DANIEL)* Eat-green-beans.

DANIEL. No, beans. 13… 12… 11…

(LENA and IRENE speak faster when they don't want Daniel to have a chance to understand, though in their excitement they may forget a time or two.)

IRENE. He's OK, right? Physically?

LENA. The doctor said if he got – y'know – erect – in his sleep, there's no physical problem.

IRENE. So?

LENA. It's weird discussing it with his sister.

IRENE. Come on, when he had to wear diapers, I changed him with you, bathed him, wiped his butt.

LENA. Yeah…well, yeah, he did, y'know, get hard.

IRENE. *(impulsively blurts out)* All right, bro!

DANIEL. No beans. *(makes Bronx cheer)* 5…4…3…2…1.

LENA. I had to see, y'know, so I tried to stay awake, but I couldn't. I woke up in the morning. I thought, it's been a nightmare. He didn't get shot. I was holding his –

*(checks **DANIEL**, resumes)*

– his, y'know, holding his cock. Y'know, I wasn't awake all the way yet…and, yeah, he was, y'know…I felt like…I got excited. This…this…like a jolt of heat. I wanted him…I wanted to…I wanted him…inside me…I put him there…but…He was looking at me trying to remember who I was.

IRENE. He knows you. He loves you.

LENA. He knows "Lena" now. A word. But not me…

*(**DANIEL** scoops up more potatoes.)*

DANIEL. "Lena."

IRENE. It's gonna come around like it was. You'll see.

LENA. Everything's hiding from him, and he can't find it.

DANIEL. Full.

(gets up)

Shit.

(He walks as though he's going to the bathroom, becomes momentarily disoriented, starts pulling down his trousers.)

Shit.

*(**LENA** and **IRENE** rush to lead him to the bathroom.)*

LENA. Danny! Wait!

IRENE. No, no, no!

DANIEL. Shit.

LENA. Bathroom! Bath – room.

IRENE. OK? Bathroom.

(They try to suppress laughter.)

DANIEL. Funny?

(frustrated anger)

Funny!

(enraged)

Funny! Funny!

LENA. No, no, no –

(He moves angrily around.)

DANIEL. Fun! Fun!

(Picks up a chair and holds it over his head like he's going to smash it, sounds of frustration, subsides.)

Shit.

IRENE. Danny…

LENA. Come on.

*(They exit with **DANIEL**. Buzzer. **IRENE** enters, crosses to intercom.)*

IRENE. Who is it?

DETECTIVE MONROE. Detective Monroe.

*(She buzzes him up. **IRENE** picks up plates. Exits. Returns with sponge. Wipes off table. Exits.)*

DANIEL. *(off stage)* Me!

LENA. *(off stage)* No!

DANIEL. *(off stage)* Yes!

(Lena comes out frustrated.)

LENA. *(loudly)* Fuck!

DANIEL. *(off stage)* Fuck…You!

LENA. Go ahead! Get in by yourself!

(to herself)

Hit your fucking head.

IRENE. *(entering)* I buzzed in the detective that's been by. He's coming up.

LENA. Tell him it'll be a minute before King Kong can see him.

*(**LENA** exits. Doorbell. **IRENE** lets in **DETECTIVE MONROE**.)*

IRENE. Danny'll be out in a minute.

DETECTIVE MONROE. How's he doing?

IRENE. A little at a time, you know? You want coffee? It's pretty fresh.

DETECTIVE MONROE. Sure.

IRENE. *(exiting)* A sec…

(stops)

It's good that you take the time to visit Danny. We appreciate it.

DETECTIVE MONROE. I'm happy to do it.

*(**IRENE** exits.)*

I see the improvement every time.

IRENE. *(off stage)* Everyday. Little by little.

DETECTIVE MONROE. He's got family around him. People that care about him. Makes a difference.

IRENE. *(off stage)* Milk?

DETECTIVE MONROE. No.

IRENE. *(off stage)* Sugar?

DETECTIVE MONROE. No.

IRENE. *(enters, coffee)* You're easy.

DETECTIVE MONROE. You make it that way.

IRENE. Detective.

DETECTIVE MONROE. What?

IRENE. You wore a wedding ring last time.

DETECTIVE MONROE. You got it wrong. I'm divorced. I wear it when I visit my mom. That sounds like, what, "preveracation." Like I'm "prevaricating," I know, but she's in assisted living. Her mind's not all there. Half the time I don't think she really knows who I am, but something like the ring, and she snaps right to it. She'd get obstreperous if she noticed I wasn't wearing it. I'd never reach the end of explaining what happened. Believe me, because she'd forget and I'd have to start all over. Oh, I'm divorced, alright. What were we talking about? Yeah, your brother's a miracle. I saw him first at trauma, all intubated. He looked likely not to make it, but he's a miracle.

IRENE. There's a long way to go.

DETECTIVE MONROE. When he's ready, the department wants to honor him. Not just a "racket." Something dignified. When he's OK with it.

IRENE. In time, I guess.

DETECTIVE MONROE. A nice buffet. Drinks.

IRENE. That'd be really nice.

DETECTIVE MONROE. Show he's appreciated.

(DANIEL enters in a sweat suit, followed by LENA.)

Mrs. Prats. I'm sorry, I should've called.

LENA. It's fine.

IRENE. I was telling him, we appreciate him visiting Danny.

DETECTIVE MONROE. *(to DANIEL)* I wanted to say hi, see how you're doing.

DANIEL. Bath.

DETECTIVE MONROE. You look better each time I see you.

LENA. *(exiting)* I'll get ready so we can go when Mara gets here.

IRENE. We're picking up my daughter.

DETECTIVE MONROE. How old is she?

IRENE. Three. Thank God for grandparents.

DETECTIVE MONROE. I have boys. 9, 11. I am divorced.

IRENE. *(raises her hand)* Single parent.

(LENA returns.)

DETECTIVE MONROE. You want to take off, I'll stay with Danny until she gets here. Mara's the Russian, right, the nurse?

LENA. He can be a handful.

DETECTIVE MONROE. Don't worry. I have a nephew who's retarded. *(beat).* Not that Danny is.

LENA. *(exiting)* I'll get my purse.

DETECTIVE MONROE. *(Beat. To* **IRENE***)* What?

IRENE. You want my cell? Y'know, in case…

(He recites it before she can write it down for him.)

DETECTIVE MONROE. 6463457539. Photographic memory. From the report. Only for numbers, though.

IRENE. Call if there's anything.

DETECTIVE MONROE. Maybe just to say, hi, sometime, if it's Ok?

IRENE. Yeah. It's Ok.

(**LENA** *returns, goes to* **DANIEL**.)

LENA. *(slowly)* I'm gonna go with Irene. Detective Monroe will stay to visit until Mara gets here. Ok? Danny?

DANIEL. Ok.

IRENE. Thank you.

DETECTIVE MONROE. It's copacetic.

(*They exit.* **DANIEL** *has mild facial tic.*)

The retarded comment came out wrong. I apologize.

(pause)

You look good. Thank God it was only 22 caliber. Any larger…fuck…I don't want to think about it. Keep positive. This isn't gonna be forever. We got a guy took one in the face a year ago that's back on the job. He gets down. We keep on him. Give him shit. So he keeps positive.

(long moment)

Detective. Look at me. A scumbag urinated on you after you were shot. He pissed in your face. Gimme a memory.

(pause)

OK. You want coffee? Danny? A cup of coffee?

DANIEL. No.

DETECTIVE MONROE. Command's gonna honor you. At least, for Merit, though, you ask me, it'll be for Valor. A ceremony down the road. Go up a grade. Something to think about.

(*There's the sound of the door opening.* **MARA** *enters.*)

We've met. I'm Detective Monroe.

MARA. I remember.

DETECTIVE MONROE. Mrs. Prats went with Irene. I was keeping Danny company until you got here.

MARA. Hi Danny. You all right?

DANIEL. Yes.

MARA. I picked up a few things.

(She puts items on table, a copy of Ghetto Cop #1, a large sketch pad, writing markers.)

DETECTIVE MONROE. Coffee's not bad. Pour you a cup?

MARA. No, thank you. Ray asked me to bring you this book.

*(**DANIEL** studies the cover art.)*

DETECTIVE MONROE. I was talking to Danny about being awarded a medal. They want to have a ceremony for him when he's ready.

DANIEL. *(sounds it out)* Ghetto Cop 1.

MARA. Danny. A medal!

DETECTIVE MONROE. Medal of Valor.

MARA. The Medal of Valor, Danny.

DETECTIVE MONROE. Good seeing you again, Detective. Hang in there. Take care.

*(**DETECTIVE MONROE** exits.)*

MARA. *(to **DANIEL**)* I'm proud for you. Medal of Valor. How do you *feel*?

DANIEL. "feel… "

MARA. To feel.

(hand to her heart)

To feel good. Proud.

DANIEL. *(mentally searching)* I don't know…"feel"…how I… What's the word… ?

(introspective)

…the word is?

(quietly to self)

...feel...

(neutral)

In my mind...I don't know feel.

MARA. *(touches her heart)* "Feel-ing."

DANIEL. ..."feel-ing? in my mind.

(to himself)

..."feel-ing" What is it?

MARA. You want to rest? I want you to try something new. With writing. You want to rest first?

DANIEL. *(opens sketch pad)* No.

MARA. I want you to try something new.

DANIEL. Write word...

MARA. No, something new.

DANIEL. Word...feel...

MARA. *(gives him marker)* You're stubborn.

DANIEL. *(writes)* Write "feel"...F-E-E-L...write "feel"... feel... feel... .

(looks unintelligible scrawls)

It's not what I see! I can't write what I see. I see some thing. I don't know what is it? I don't know what it's called? I don't know what it means! What I knew. I don't know.

MARA. Danny.

DANIEL. *(exiting)* Fuck you!

MARA. Come sit down. Don't be pussy! A Russian soldier. Zasetsky. Had injury worse than you! Half his brain. He learned he could write if he didn't think about it. He couldn't read it. His own words. Then – good things came. He wrote book of struggle. He never gave up. He curse God. But he never give up! You have scratch compared to Russian soldier Zasetsky! Get pussy ass in here!

(He returns –)

DANIEL. You have no idea! Nightmare life!

MARA. You will wake up. Don't give up. *(beat)* Come sit down, sit down and look at me.

(He sits at the table. She puts the pad in front of him.)

Don't think about what you write. Writing is built in memory. In arm. In hand. Put pen on the page. Put it on the page! Look at me. Look at clown Mara from Russia.

(makes face)

Let hand move. Don't think "what." A different memory…built in…Arm. Hand. Auto-ma-tic. Yes? Auto-ma-tic.

DANIEL. Auto-ma-tic.

(She makes faces, as he writes, looking at her, and repeating softly, "auto-ma-tic," eventually draining off, as he continues to write. Music.)

Scene 18

(148th st. **DELROY**, *a blanket around his shoulders. Crack. Walks down street.)*

DELROY. *(sing song; quietly to himself. Like child's limerick)*
Dead now. Dead now.
Homey put lead in the head of an undercover narc.
Homey put lead in the head of an undercover narc.
Dead now. He dead now.

(music; blues scream)

Dead on the ground.
Blood on the ground.

(sing song; quietly, like child limerick)

Dead now. He dead now.

(music; blues scream)

Shot in the heart by the undercover narc.

(sing song.)

Dead now. He dead now.

(Exits.)

Scene 19

*(Front room. **RAY** is in a better grade security guard uniform. **DANIEL** reads from "Ghetto Cop 3." **RAY** helps out. Each have copies of book. **LENA** is in the recliner looking at a large writing pad of **DANIEL**'s.)*

DANIEL. "The nigga wanted to know how it… "

RAY. "Felt."

DANIEL. " – to die and now he did. He was another dead rapper. The same… "

RAY. "dead"

DANIEL. " – as everybody else. Dead at the wheel of a new… ca…

RAY. Ca-dil-lac

DANIEL. Cadillac… Es… Es…

RAY. Es-ca-lade.

DANIEL. Es-calade. "But still dead in the ghetto. Ah… "the na… " Don't tell me – "…naked fox was standing at the door waiting. The next thing, we were slamming. I had worse pussy, for a ghetto cop, a lot worse."

RAY. "I had worse pussy, for a Ghetto Cop, a lot worse." Ghetto Cop #3. My kind of story. Ghetto Cop don't mess around. Y'readin' good.

LENA. Your writing is better too. I can read it now. I don't understand how you write it but can't read it.

DANIEL. Built in.

RAY. Yrright. And the rest will come.

DANIEL. Built in memory. Writing.

RAY. I think cuz it's written in long hand. What do you call it? Cur…cur?

DANIEL. Cur-sive.

RAY. There y'go.

LENA. I don't understand how he can write it and can't –

DANIEL. *(cuts in, sharply)* Cur-sive.

LENA. I know but –

DANIEL. Cursive!

LENA. Don't yell at me! I'm trying to understand!

RAY. It's good, though, Danny feels it – and can say it. His feelin. It's good, Lena, he has a feelin' about it. It's good, Danny, y'do.

DANIEL. Thanks.

RAY. I gotta go guard stacks of plywood now. Make sure nobody puts any in their pockets.

LENA. I filled the thermos.

RAY. Oh, yeah? You the best.

(to DANIEL)

Y'know that, she the best?

DANIEL. ...*is*.

RAY. Huh?

DANIEL. She *is* the best. Not *she* the best.

RAY. Y'hangin' with that fool Monroe too muthafuken much, but arright. Important thing, we agree how good she is. She *is* the best.

(exiting)

I'm a nigga can learn.

LENA. Danny? You want me to read what you wrote?

DANIEL. OK.

LENA. "Dark night bright light fright ... m-o- I think it's mo- mo- ... "

RAY. *(enters with thermos)* Arright. I'm gone.

DANIEL. OK.

LENA. Mo-b del Roy? Danny?

RAY. *(stops)* Delroy?

LENA. Mo B Del Roy or...?

RAY. Did'y'ax me about some Delroy?

DANIEL. "Del-roy."

RAY. First time you was by the VA, some Delroy?

DANIEL. Delroy?

RAY. Yeah.

DANIEL. I don't remember.

RAY. Yeah. Delroy, 151?

DANIEL. No.

RAY. Arright. Must've dreamt it. You're on your way aren't you? You're on your way. *(pause)* Yeah.

(to **LENA***)*

I forgot to mention I have somethin' after work.

LENA. I'm off, so no problem.

RAY. Arright then.

(**RAY** *exits. Looking back at room before doing so.* **LENA** *caresses* **DANIEL.**)

LENA. I'm sorry I yelled. I love you.

DANIEL. *(hugs her)* Hard.

LENA. I understand. I'm sorry.

DANIEL. *(lifting her)* No. Me.

LENA. Oh…

DANIEL. For you. Wife. She the best.

Scene 20

(Loading dock. **RAY** *approaches* **DELROY**.*)*

DELROY. Whatcha want?

RAY. Whatcha got?

DELROY. Whatcha need, nigga?

RAY. Y'Delroy?

DELROY. Who?

RAY. Nigga told me Delroy up about 151.

DELROY. Naw. Go on. I'm workin'.

RAY. Y'shits good, B?

DELROY. You buyin or cryin?

RAY. I heard Delroy's shit good.

DELROY. Y'crying.

RAY. Gimme a jumbo.

*(***DELROY*** gives* **RAY** *a vial for his 20.)*

DELROY. That the daddy.

RAY. Delroy suppose to be up around 151

DELROY. Y'like a cop. Y'a fake cop. A rent-a-cop cop.

RAY. Bullshit job.

DELROY. This is 148. 4-8th a world of difference. Y'stay steady, I hear any Delroy, I let y'know.

RAY. Arright. Y'shit good. I be back. Whatcha name?

DELROY. People call me Killa because of my raps. Killa Crisis.

*(***RAY*** starts off, turns back.)*

RAY. Killa, y'got a nickel stem to sell?

DELROY. Not no new one for a nickel.

RAY. Any pipe a pipe.

*(***RAY*** buys the pipe. Crosses stage slowly.)*

DELROY. *(to himself)* Go like, lookit, mom, listen up…

(Lights stay up on **DELROY** *at loading dock as they come*

up on a storage yard gate. **DELROY** *hits the pipe.*)

DELROY. *(continued) (to himself)* Y'think I'm with ya, but I'm in my mind lookin for a word…ice…Ice in my diamond mine. Diamond mine…dia-mind…in my mind…ice…die mind

(**RAY** *crosses to lumber yard chair and trash barrel. Tosses crack into barrel. Sits. Struggles. Gets up and digs in barrel. Comes up with crack vial. Sits in folding chair. Struggles. Loads pipe and smokes.*)

RAY. *(loads and fires up pipe)* Oh, man… oh… I don't know… whatcha doing? Whatcha doing?

(hits pipe)

Shit. oh…where have y'been…shit talks…shit talking to me…where y'been? Whatcha say? I hear ya, Where y'been. Ray? I hear ya. I don't know. Don't know where? Here I am. Here I am now.

(Music.)

Scene 21

(Front room. **LENA** *and* **MARA**, *dressed up.* **LENA** *enters from rear rolling the TV. She's not dressed)*

IRENE. What Danny say?

LENA. He said, "Ray's alive, there's hope." I'd better kick the man of the hour out of the bathroom so I can get ready.

IRENE. Just give Ray 10 bucks for the TV. That's all he'll get.

LENA. I don't want it.

DANIEL. *(off stage)* Lena! Come please.

*(**LENA** exits.)*

(Buzzer. **IRENE** *goes to intercom.)*

IRENE. Who is it?

RAY. *(V.O.) (intercom)* It's Ray.

(She buzzes him up.)

IRENE. When's the last time you saw him?

MARA. Two months.

IRENE. If he stole my money, my credit cards and my jewlery, his ass would be in Rikers.

MARA. Today's for Danny.

(Doorbell. **IRENE** *lets* **RAY** *in. His security guard uniform has gone seriously downhill, like him.)*

RAY. Damn but don't y'all look good.

IRENE. Danny's getting honored today. Medal of Valor.

RAY. Arright. Yeah. OK. I'm jis gonna tip on out with the TV. I know what y'thinkin, y'not wrong, but...

IRENE. Take the TV and go.

RAY. I just need to finish up somethin I'm doin.

*(**DANIEL** comes from the rear. He wears dress uniform pants, barefoot. Dress shirt.)*

DANIEL. Cutter...

RAY. Well...y'gettin your medal? That's good.

DANIEL. Thanks.

RAY. Bring y'luck. You'll see. Mine's kept me from some bad shit. I'm gettin back, y'know, to the VA. I know I got to do it, soon, be soon.

MARA. These are words.

RAY. I gotta to do this, to do this other thing, for now, somethin else, y'know. For now. Well... Medal of Valor. That's good. Shit, that tops me.

(RAY *picks up the TV.* LENA *enters in a dress for the ceremony.*)

(*to* LENA) Hi, ah, well...

DANIEL. Don't give up.

RAY. Arright

DANIEL. You didn't then.

RAY. Arright.

DANIEL. You saved them.

RAY. ...y'rememberin things now?

DANIEL. I remember that day in dessert.

RAY. Yeah...arright...

(*He exits with TV.*)

LENA. You should finish getting dressed.

DANIEL. OK.

(DANIEL *exits rear. Buzzer.* IRENE *goes to the intercom.*)

IRENE. Who is it?

DETECTIVE MONROE. (*V.O.*) (*over intercom*) Richard. You people ready?

(MARA *turns away.* IRENE *goes to the intercom.*)

IRENE. Almost. Come up.

DETECTIVE MONROE. (*V.O*) (*muffled intercom*) Where you going with that?

RAY. (*V.O.*) (*muffled intercom*) This is mine. Ask 'em, shit.

IRENE. (*overlapping VOs*) What's going on? Richard. Let him go. It's his. The TV's his. Come up.

(She buzzes him up.)

LENA. *(calls, to rear)* Detective Monroe's here. How you doing?

DANIEL. *(offstage)* Fucking coat buttons!

(LENA exits.)

IRENE. You Ok?

MARA. Yeah. Phew. Ok.

*(**DETECTIVE MONROE** enters. **IRENE** kisses him.)*

DETECTIVE MONROE. Sorry about that.

*(**DANIEL** enters with **LENA**. He wears dress uniform. Hat in hand. Puts on hat, a grin to **DETECTIVE MONROE**.)*

(Music.)

Scene 22

*(Riverside park. Dark granite tunnel underpass. **DELROY** and **RAY** are hitting the pipe. **DELROY**'s appearance has deteriorated. There's a shopping cart with a few pieces of sorry crap in it. A couple cardboard boxes with **RAY**'s possessions, not much of anything visible.)*

RAY. Does that guy stay in your tunnel?

DELROY. He be here sometime.

RAY. What wuz the shit on the space ships that nigga was sayin?

DELROY. Y'was there.

RAY. Yeah, I know, but, shit…Space ships, that's some shit. Nigga saw them on TV?

DELROY. Y'gotta slow the shit down, the nigga said, the same shit they showed on the TV, but y'slow down that shit, down to slo-mo, y'see the space ships. They like fly around.

RAY. So, space ships did it?

DELROY. The planes did it. The fucked up Iraq al queda niggas did it. The space ships fly around lookin' at what crazy niggas do down here. I'm gonna put it in my rap to flavor my shit. My man do beats – fuck's my nigga's name? Fa…fa…?

RAY. Keep the first part in your mind. Y'see the fa…fa… while ya –

DELROY. *(cutting in)* What the fuck y' talkin about?

RAY. Y'tryin t'say some – !

DELROY. I'm sayin' he do my beats! I let go free style – Fat Spanky! That's my nigga's name. Fat Spanky gonna lay beats for me. Know what I'm sayin? Word, nigga! Let all that fly, space ships, rock, haze, po-po pigs, pussy, dome, chrome, timbos, 3 dice, cars, Harlem, Hennessey, ice – all that shit – work it all! Cuz everyone gonna get killed, we know that …

*(**DELROY** hits the pipe. **RAY** takes out his medal, rubs*

it.)

RAY. I got good luck though. S'my good luck piece.

DELROY. It work, huh?

RAY. Keep the pipe from tearin' up the Wernicke area of my mind. It do, y'don't watch it.

DELROY. What happen'd?

RAY. This shit tear up the Wernicke area, y'don't watch it.

DELROY. What the fuck you talkin' about?

RAY. The Wernicke area. Called the Wernicke area. Part'a y'brain. The Wernicke part get fucked up, y'talk shit'n don't make sense. Y'don't know ABC. Y'don't know A-E – O – y'know – I.O.U. That the vowel sounds, nigga. Y too sometimes. Y'can't remember human language y'Wernicke get fucked up. That's why you see nigga's walkin' behind shoppin' carts, talkin' pigeon talk to fucked up invisible pigeons that ain't there. They feed 'em too. Nigga be breakin' up a roll too hard for his fucked up teeth and feedin' invisible pigeons talkin to em in pigeon talk. Real pigeons come along, he scare them off. Don't want them eatin' the food he feed his invisible pigeons.

DELROY. Y'already fucked up. Y'already a shoppin' cart nigga.

RAY. I got my TV in my luggage, muthafucka. Right there in my luggage.

DELROY. Uh-huh…yeah, sure, nigga.

RAY. I got luggage. I got shit hidin' my TV! I don't want no nigga stealin' my TV. I have to take my TV down around 116th, n'sell it to some downtown college nigga. Y'got to get down of 2-5th. Y'stay uptown nothin' but broke – What the word?…fuck is it… y'know broke nigga program they on? "s" word…government program…sec… shu… "section 8!" Nothin but section 8 niggas. Y'get bout 10 dollars s'all. Y'go downtown, y'know, 1-16 t'bout 1-10, 'bout the college there, 'bout Columbia College there, they rich there, sell it to a downtown nigga you get 30 dollars. Y'get more y'don't hurry, maybe 50. Shit cable ready. 300 channels. I get myself together first, I go on down.

(hits pipe)

Y'name Delmont, ain't it?

DELROY. Killa Crisis. Name I record my shit. Name people know me.

RAY. Someone somewhere, I met was Delmont. No doubt.

(hits pipe)

...so be it.

(climbs the high)

Vooowwwweeelllls...!!!! aaaaaaa...eeeeeee...

(bigger)

iiiiiii...ooooooo...uuuuuuuu...

(**DELROY** *hits him on the head.* **RAY** *crumbles.*)

DELROY. Talkin shit y'don't know.

(searches **RAY***)*

What y'have is mine...big little young old...it mine... man woman...

(discards medal)

Good luck? Shit. Y'fake luck. I'm Killa Crisis. Y'ain't nothin. Nothin. Y'shit ain't nothin.

(exiting with cart)

Y'aint nothin, nothin, y'ain't nothin...

RAY. *(crawls)* Help...someone...Help.

(Music.)

Scene 23

(Lights up on **DANIEL** *at mic as* **DETECTIVE MONROE** *pins metal on him.* **DETECTIVE MONROE** *exits.)*

DANIEL. I want to thank Lena. My wife. Irene. My sister. Ray. Mara. My friends…umm…Detective Monroe…I want to thank all of you here. I want to say…I want to say. Don't give up. No matter what.

(Music.)

Scene 25

(Riverside park. Dark granite tunnel underpass. RAY pulls himself toward the tunnel exit. Reaches dim light at exterior.)

RAY. Help…please…I need help.

(Fade to black. Music.)

The End

Also by
Bob Glaudini...

The Identical Same Temptation
Dutch Heart of Man
Jack Goes Boating

Please visit our website **samuelfrench.com** for complete descriptions and licensing information

www.ingramcontent.com/pod-product-compliance
Lightning Source LLC
Chambersburg PA
CBHW070648300426
44111CB00013B/2327